1. Abergele Road, Penmaenrhos, c.1915

The road has been widened and all the buildings on the left demolished. They were, from L-R: Uwch-y-Don Farm (with it's kitchen below the level of the road) and Voryn Isa and Voryn Hall Holiday Camp. The Bryn Heli cul-de-sac now occupies much the same area. Local people used to buy their milk from inside the low building on the left. Miners Lane meets the road from top right and Tan-y-Wal leaves it round the corner at top left. The buildings on the horizon are the semi-detached houses, Bay View and Craigfryn, numbers 478 and 480 Abergele Road.

2. Rose Cottages, Penmaenrhos, 1915.

L-R: Margaret Williams and her sons Trevor (who became the *North Wales Weekley News* reporter 'Cormorant') and John, her mother and father, Hannah and John Jones. The cottages were demolished so that the road (supported on concrete slits) leading to the Colwyn Bay Hotel could be built.

3. D. O. Roberts, Butcher, Penmaenrhos, c.1920

This building and business have now both gone, victims of the road widening scheme at Penmaenrhos. The shop stood near the entrance to Miners Lane, opposite the present-day Brownlie's shop (505 Abergele Road). Mr D. O. Roberts (left) had his own slaughter house which was located under Brownlie's on Tan-y-Wal, where the blood of the animals flowed down the road and the workers smoked cigarettes while they worked!

Introduction

If a man or woman, in 1997, were to contemplate the passage of ten generations of his ancestors, he would discover that he had one thousand and twenty four of them forming what Osbert Sitwell described as a 'cloud of witnesses'. These witnesses to the development of our town are I trust present in these slim volumes of nostalgia. History is a babble of voices which need to be interpreted, for memory, is finally, all we own.

In 1909, Lloyd George asked: 'Who made ten thousand people owners of the soil, and the rest of us trespassers in the land of our birth'. Just after the Great War, ten years after Lloyd George posed his question, perhaps a quarter of the land of England and Wales changed hands. Colwyn Bay was a perfect example of those changing times and, from a crescent and sweep of land maintained by a wealthy family and the Church, it was transformed into a town run by people who owned their own homes and ran their own businesses. The democratic age as we know it had arrived.

Before 1865, fields and woods swept down to the water's edge and the area had been stirred from it's pastoral calm only by the tramp of passers-by; the Romans laying siege to the Druids in Anglesey, invading armies of Saxons and Normans forcing their way westwards, Welsh forces moving east to stem a breach in border defences—all moving elsewhere, and disregarding the Bay itself. Only one event from British history took place within the district, the capture of King Richard II by Bolingbroke's men at the foot of Penmaenhead. The building of turnpike roads, which began in the 1760s, slowly improved communications, but it was the construction of the railway in 1848 which heralded dramatic change. By 1901 the population had grown to 8,689, a mixture of English and Welsh people together forming a bustling seaside community.

This volume, and it's predecessors, are a search for what Henry James called 'the visitable past'. The pictures are laid out as before to indicate a journey from Old Colwyn to Rhos-on-Sea and I have been helped along the way by a willing and chattering group of people. Elsie Baugh, Louisa Cheadle (now aged 106 and in excellent form), Ken Davies (Edenfield, Penmaenrhos), Geoffrey Edwards (the former Town Clerk), Gillian Fraser and her staff at Colwyn Bay Library, Joan Humphreys of Shawforth, Rhona Kinghorn, John Neal (son of Johnnie Neal and May Berry), Ron Sifleet and Harold Sims of Letchworth have all been particularly helpful. Along the way I have been waylaid by many old friends who have been happy to chat to me about the old days.

Graham Roberts
Rhos-on-Sea
1997

BIBLIOGRAPHY

Bradley, A. G.	*Highways and Byways in North Wales*	Macmillan, 1919
Brockbank, H. M.	Notes on sixteen lectures on the History of Colwyn Bay given by Norman Tucker	Privately printed, 1952
Crean, Patrick J.	*A Life of the Venerable William Davies, Catholic Martyr*	Catholic Trust Soc. 1958
Davies, Joan M.	*Llysfaen, Our Village* (Vols 1-6)	1992
Jones, I. W.	'Luftwaffe Over Clwyd'	Denbighshire Historical Society Transactions, 1977
Jones, J. R.	*The Welsh Builders on Merseyside*	J. R. Jones, Cintra, 1946
Matthews, Gwenda M.	*Colwyn Bay Community Hospital: A History*	Colwyn Bay Hospital League of Friends, 1994
Mellor, George E.	*Colwyn Bay Cricket Club: A History*	Colwyn Bay Cricket Club, 1992
Miller, J.	*Old Colwyn English Baptist Church*	Privately printed, 1993
Mottershead, A. L.	*Hitherto-Always: A History of Ebenezer Chapel, Rhiw Road*	Colwyn Duplicating Service, 1978
Parry, Parch. T. & Jones, T. M.	*Methodistiaeth yn Nosbarth Colwyn Bay*	E. W. Evans, 1909
Price, John	*Old Price's Remains*	Virtue Bros., 1864
Smith, Henry	*Bureaucrats in Battle Dress: The History of the Ministry of Food Home Guard*	R. E. Jones, 1945
Thomas, Dilys	*Old Colwyn from Small Beginnings*	1993
Weaver, Mike	*Alvin Langdon Coburn: Symbolist Photographer*	An Apeture Monograph, 1986
Ysgol Cystennin Pupils	*Young Persons Guide to the History of Colwyn Bay*	1991

4. Marine Road, Old Colwyn, 1974

The railway on the left, *Colwyn Bay Hotel* on the skyline and the Tan Llan Post Office at the far end of the row of houses. Both road and houses have now gone, replaced by the A55 dual-carriageway through Colwyn Bay. By the lamp-post was the entrance to Roseberry Avenue (cul-de-sac).

5. Fron Terrace, Old Colwyn, 1910

This was the main road through Old Colwyn. Opposite these houses was Bryn Ffynnon Terrace. There used to be a natural dip in the land (still visible where the allotments are beside Old Colwyn methodist Church) forcing the road to take a route down from Peulwys Road, behind what is now Meredith & Kirkham's garage, across Wellington Road and so in front of Fron Terrace.

6. Dolwen Road, c.1920

Dolwen Road can be seen at middle left, concealed by hedges. The buildings (R-L) are: Pentre Isa (now a residential home); Whiteacres (now on Llanelian Heights); Bryn Awel (125 Llanelian Rd); Bryn Awel Gardens (the low shed –see Vol 2 , picture 10); Arosfa (18 Dolwen Road) and the cottage at top left (known as Clwt) demolished to make way for three bungalows on the left as you rise up Llanelian Road, just below the Vicarage. Miss Villey (thought by locals to be descended from French aristocracy) lived at Clwt. She reputedly never washed but swam every day in the sea off Tan Llan. She wrote a book of poems entitled, *Brief Bits of Buffoonery About Birds and Beasts.*

7. St Catherines's Church, Old Colwyn, c.1925

Built in 1837 as a Chapel of Ease to Llandrillo, the church gained it's own parish in 1844. The land on which the church was built was given by Mr John Lloyd Wynne of Coed Coch and the Rev. John Boulger. The clock in the church tower was installed in 1890 in memory of the Rev. J. D. Jones, vicar 1866-87. The tram lines which can be seen in the road carried trams as far as the Queens Hotel, Old Colwyn.

8. Marine Terrace, Old Colwyn, c.1914

Today, the Marine Hotel and the roundabout at the end of Holyrood Avenue and Llanelian Road are located at the end of this terrace. The central house (No 244) is now the premises of Pickerings Newsagents but in the late 1930s was the Bedford Commercial Hotel and Café run by Mr & Mrs Rawlings. Mrs Rawlings sold a cup of tea for $1/2$d every day to the staff of the Red Garages on the opposite side of the road.

9. Min-y-Don Cottages, Old Colwyn, c.1920

These semi-detached cottages, at the bottom of Beach Road, were built in about 1860 on the site of Sir Richard Butler Clough's old coal yard and were then called Glan-y-Môr Cottages. At that time, Edward and Mary Williams and their eight children lived in the right hand cottage and ran the sweet shop on the right of the photograph. The cottages were sometimes marooned by the high tides and could only be reached by boat.

10. Colwyn Town band, 1928

The band is photographed in Princes Road, Old Colwyn, outside the Baptist Church where they used one of the rooms for practices. The bandsmen are (L-R):

Back row: A. Conway; T. Davies; D. Stevens; unknown; W. E. Davies; T. Newell; J. Conway; unknown; W. Newell; J. Watson; W. Parry.

Middle row: S. Scott; W. Conway; A. Hughes; J. Cullaton; E. Conway; W. Reckless; C. Hughes; unknown; W. Heap; Jim Conway.

Seated: Unknown; unknown; Llew Conway; Cllr Davies; unknown; Mr Woolford; David Edwards; D. Jones; Theophilus Jones; George Conway.

Front row: Dick Jones; Idris Williams.

11. The Blessed William Davies, 1556-93

Born at Groes-yn-Eirias, near the present entrance to Eirias Park, William Davies was admitted to the seminary at Rheims, France in 1582 and ordained a priest in April 1585. Harsh anti-Catholic laws had been instituted and there were government spies throughout England and Wales. On 6 June 1585, in secret and probably disguised, Davies returned to Colwyn to minister to the local people. Eight years later, on 15 March 1592, he was arrested and imprisoned at Beaumaris where, in July 1593, he was hanged, drawn and quartered, becoming the first Welsh martyred priest. His last words were 'They yoke, O Lord, is sweet and Thy burden light'. The plaque shown here is in Our Lady Queen of Martyrs Church, Beaumaris

12. Eirias Dingle, c.1899

These cottages (now 1–6 Nant Eirias) still stand beside the Groes River. Today, Eirias Park is just over the bank at the back of the cottages and Bryn-y-Maen can be seen in the background. The pathway joins the Dingle cul-de-sac which is entered from Abergele Road, opposite the Park Hotel and, if one followed the river upstream for about half a mile you would come to Mr Greenfield's smithy at Groes Mill.

13. Colwyn Bay Hospital, 1905

Built of red brick, this was the original hospital building erected by public subscription in 1898. The doorway in the picture is still the main entrance into the hospital. The first subscription made to the hospital was for £100 from Mr & Mrs Francis Nunn who donated a further £200 in 1920. The field in the foreground is now the site of the hospital wards. In 1926 this field was presented to the hospital board by Mrs Fred Stott of Plas Parciau.

14. Tyn-y-Maes, 1915

In the early part of the present century, there were fourteen privately run schools in Colwyn Bay. Ty'n-y-Maes housed the Dingle Wood Boys School. This building later became a guest house (run by Mr William Shoesmith) and was burnt down in 1953. The headmaster of the Dingle Wood School was Mr James Wood, MA, JP who lived at No 20 Lawson Road. The school gym, later converted into 'The Bungalow' by the late Ald. Len Frith, is located a short distance from the present-day *Edelweiss Hotel*.

15. L. A. Little, The Creamery, c.1935

Located on the corner of Lawson Rd and Abergele Rd. Each evening (the shop remained open until 10pm) Lady Adelaide Eva Erskine would come here in her long black dress and blue veil, to buy three table jellies which she would give to her dogs, Piggy, Floundy and Gertie. She lived as a recluse at The Nest (now No 56 Llanelian Road). She died on 3 September 1938 and was buried in Llanelian Cemetery. In 1941, appropriately enough, The Nest was the residence of a Mrs Heron.

16. Maelgwyn Fish, Game & Poultry Stores, 1898

The owners, Mr & Mrs Frank Madren with their sons Harold and George (right) and two helpers (left). This building is now Nos 76 and 78 Abergele Rd. Mr Madren had previously been a builder and his initials can be seen on the buildings between Toad Hall Inn and Sea Bank Road. In 1892 he built what is now the Balmoral Holiday Flats and in 1893 what is now the Majestic Grill and Contin-ental

17. Midland Garage, Abergele Road, c.1925

This garage was located on the corner of Erw Wen Road and Abergele Road in the East End of Colwyn Bay. In 1930, it was bought by a Mr Braid who owned the Abergele Motor Company in Abergele and he renamed it 'Braid's Garage'. The name Midland lingered on for many years as the Midland Cash Stores (ironmongery) which was located next-door but one along Abergele Road.

After the Second World War, Mr Braid saw the coming attraction for the middle classes of owning a motor car and set up his own finance company to help this process along.

18. Corner Erw Wen Road and Abergele Road, 1930

This site is now occupied by the Stermat hardware Shop (and once the premises of Braid's Garage). The gentleman in the centre of the photograph is Mr J. R. Morris, a director of the Colwyn Bay and District Advertising and Billposting Co. The poster on the extreme left is for Barnum & Bailey's Greatest Show on Earth. The corrugated building in the background is the first English Baptist Church.

19. J. Boardman's China Shop, c.1909

This shop was located at what is now No 53 Abergele Road. On the left can just be seen the side of Tabernacle Chapel (see Vol 2, No 15). Board-man's business was established in Derby in 1880 before moving to Colwyn Bay. The shop eventually closed in 1979 by which time it was located in Penrhyn Road. The building seen here was built in 1904 and the proprietor, Mr James Boardman (1834-1911), is standing at the door. The sign above his head reads: 'Goods packed by exper-ienced packer'.

20. G. Marfell, Ironmongers, Abergele Road, c.1905

This building (Nos 63 & 65 Abergele Road) is now occupied by three businesses, The Tandoori Curry House, Alexander Locksmiths and, on the first floor, Dawson Solicitors. All the drain pipes which you see in the photograph are still in place today. The person standing second from the right is Mr Rhys Powell Bowen, whose wife was a nursemaid to the Marfell children. Mr Rhys Powell's sons were William J. Bowen and Stewart Powell Bowen MBE, founders of the Colwyn Bay architectural firm of Bowen Dan Davies & Co.

21. Plas Tirion, 1939

This building (constructed around 1895) was once a school for girls run by Miss Whitehouse. It then became the Colwyn Bay Maternity Home and was opened as such by Ald. Miss E. M. Hovey, JP, CC (Chairman of the Maternity and Child Welfare Committee) on Friday 14 July 1939. The building still stands on the corner of Nant-y-Glyn Road and Nant-y-Glyn Avenue and is now used by Clwydian Community Care.

22. Colwyn Bay Brotherhood, 1908

This was an interdenominational group which usually met in the Old Colwyn methodist Church. The photograph shows the members on a picnic at Bryn Gwenallt, Abergele on 4 July, 1908. Miss Florrie Greenfield was presented with a trophy for singing for the Brotherhood.

23. Colwyn Bay, 1899

This photograph (part of a much larger panoramic view of Colwyn Bay) was taken from the roof of the partially constructed first pier. The pit —originally called 'The Ballast Pit'— from which the material for the railway embankment was excavated is visible behind the railway in front of Sea View Terrace. In those days it formed an unofficial playground for children. The area was eventually used as the railway goods yard and for coal storage. This is now the site of the Colwyn Centre shopping precinct. The Pat Collins Fun Fair was located just the other side of the railway bridge.

24. Railway Station Forecourt, c.1960

All the buildings in this photograph (Railway Enquiries Office, Colwyn Bay Information Bureau and the Station frontage) have gone. This area was dug up during the 1970s and the A55 Expressway now runs beneath the present forecourt. The station once boasted four tracks. The first Station Master was a Mr George and a house called Pen-y-Bryn (now demolished) was built on the station forecourt to accommodate Irish labourers engaged on the Penmaenhead tunnel construction. The lower part of this property was used as drinking vaults.

25. East Parade, c.1960

The whole of this road, and the houses, were cleared to make way for the A55 Expressway. The Belvedere Hotel (see Vol 2, Nos 59 & 60) is in the centre of the picture and the Pendorlan Secondary Modern School and the Wireless College were sited at the far end of the road. The railway is off to the left and you can now drive off the A55 to an interchange which is situated off to the bottom right of the photograph.

26. The Pork Shop, 1910

Mostyn's butchers was located in the building which now houses White's Radio (No 42 Abergele Road), opposite the Tabernacle Chapel. The man on the right is the co-owner, Mr Robert Mostyn who in those days, as can be seen, was not much troubled by health and hygiene regulations.

27. Davies Brothers, Butchers, c.1918

The two figures and the prize winning cattle are standing in front of 103a Abergele Road (now Health 2000), on the corner of Back Belgrave Road. The outward appearance of the premises have changed little in the nearly 80 years since this photograph was taken. The man on the right is Robert Mostyn of the Colwyn Bay Pork Shop

28. Colwyn Bay Hockey Team, 1906

The team is posing in what is now the Coach Park opposite the Norfolk House Hotel on Princes Drive. The cone shaped tower which can be seen in the background is on Selby Towers. Ten years previously, the press reported that a Ladies v Gentlemen cricket match at Colwyn Bay resulted in the Ladies winning by 67 runs to 60, the Gentlemen having to bat with broomsticks and field left-handed.

29. Colwyn Bay Royal Welch Fusiliers Darts Team, 1960

The team members are (L-R):

Back row: Bert Jones; Howie Griffiths; Joe Cross.

Middle row: Vick Hughes; Walter Davies; David Jones (son of Bert); Mr Sifleet; Ken Hayes; Bob Hughes (brother of Vick).

Front row: Billy Wynn; Dave Fairclough; Geoff Jones (Capt.); Tom Lloyd; Cliff Baker; Bill Thomas.

30. Elianus Boarding Establishment, 1929

This building is sited on the corner of Rhiw Bank and Abergele Road looking across at Greenfield Road. Mrs A. M. Griffiths, the proprietress offered a 'liberal table and home comforts'. The shop was the premises of Dyson & Wilkinson. Originally built by the son of the lighthouse-keeper at Point Lynus on Anglesey and the house took its name from the latin Elianus (St Elian or Lynus).

31. Victoria Avenue, c.1920

The carriage and horses are part of a May Queen procession (Queen Hesha) going down Victoria Avenue towards the railway station. The low buildings behind the tree on the right are part of the coal and goods yard where the Colwyn centre is now situated. The field later became the site of Catlin's fun fair. The tall building on the left is the Mount Melleray Hotel (run by Mrs E. Holt and Miss A. B. Richardson) and is now one of only three buildings remaining in what is left of the avenue. Leading round to the right is Greenfield Road.

32. Capel Cyntaf, c.1880

The Welsh Presbyterian Chapel, the first church to be built in Colwyn Bay, stood opposite the present site of the Midland Bank on Conway Road. It's foundation can be traced to a thatched cottage known as Tŷ'n-y-ffordd, which stood on the turnpike almost opposite the present day Belgrave Road, where, in the 1840s, there were informal meetings and a Sunday school. The church cost £700 to build and was opened in May 1873 when it was jointly used by the Welsh and English community. The back wall of this building can still be seen incorporated into the present structure.

33. Woodland Road East, c.1929

This photograph was taken from Woodland Road East, looking at the corner of the road with Abergele Road, where the building (which once housed Waterworth Brothers fruit stores) is being demolished to make way for F. W. Woolworth's Bazaar.

34. Sergeants, Royal Welsh Fusiliers, 1895

Members of the 2nd Volunteer Battalion, Royal Welsh Fusiliers (the spelling was changed to Welch in 1920). The Rifle Volunteer Corps of the mid-19th century became affiliated to the Royal Welsh Fusiliers in 1884. In 1908 they became part of the 4th Battalion, Royal Welsh Fusiliers Territorial Force.

The figures are, L-R: Colour Sergeant Burwell, Sergeants T. Morgan, T. Homan (fancy goods dealer, The Regent, Conway Road), Evans, Joseph William Adamson (chemist, Station Road and future Chairman of Colwyn Bay Urban District Council, 1930-31) and T. Brackstone (estate agent, Central Chambers, Abergele Road).

35. The Bay, c.1905

The three large houses to the left of the tree are Nos 8 (Holmleigh), 4 (Velindra) and 15 (Wolverton) Woodland Park. The track entering the photograph from the right is now the line taken by Hillside Road. The spire on the left is St John's Methodist Church. The large building above the tree is the Colwyn Bay Hotel and the spire to its right is the English Presbyterian Church. The field is now covered by houses on York Road, Hillside Road, Woodhill Road, Coed Pella Road and Claughton Road.

36. Boots Chemist, March 1953

This was, and still is, Branch No 253. The business is now conducted from premises in Station Road and this building, 21 Conway Road, is now used by Tandy & Co. The premises to the right (now the Nationwide Building Society) were built for Barclays Bank, with an under-sized turret, to house a club as well as a bank. It was along this road in 1901 that the procession accompanied the three returning Volunteers from the Boer War. The *Welsh Coast Pioneer* reported that "...the band struck up a lively quickstep and followed by an excited throng, proceeded ...to the quarters of the Regiment".

37. Rydal School, c.1910

This photograph was taken before the school chapel (the present dining room) was built. Originally called Rydal Mount, the school was founded in 1885 under the headmastership of Mr T. G. Osborn, MA. The original fifteen pupils were housed and taught in the building on the left which is partially concealed by a tree. By 1890, there were 100 pupils and the extension on the right was built. A pupil of those days wrote that the railway tunnel "beyond Old Colwyn was known as 'the prison gate', and when we passed through it after holidays we were in our own little world."

The school now caters for day pupils and boarders and for girls as well as boys.

38. Rydal School Cricket Team 1st XI, 1931

Edgar Bibby (Capt — seated centre); D. L. Hughes (standing extreme left); Roy Wooller (standing extreme right); Wilfred Wooller (seated second from left).

Wilf Wooller was born at Rhos-on-Sea in 1912. He won three Cambridge rugby Blues (1933-5), two cricket Blues (1935-6) and played centre-forward for Cardiff City in 1939. He was capped 18 times for Wales at rugby, played squash for Wales and cricket for Denbighshire and Glamorgan (1938-62)—captaining the latter from 1947-60). He was Secretary of Glamorgan CCC from 1947-77 and a Test Selector from 1955-61. He also played rugby for the Army (scoring three tries against France in 1940), Cardiff, Sale, London Welsh and the Barbarians. He was a regular sports commentator on BBC Wales and had several columns in national daily newspapers. He died in 1996.

39. Rotary Gymnastic & Athletic Club, 1925

This photograph was taken outside the gym at Rydal School. All the club members were local Colwyn Bay men who were trained by Sergeant Major Wilde (formerly of the Royal Welch Fusiliers) who also trained the Rydal School Officer Training Corps.

40. Princes Drive, 1904

This photograph was taken where the road crosses Marine Road. The 'Ivy Lea' plaque on the corner is still in place 90 years later (a reminder of the original Ivy Lea Hotel run by the Misses Groves). All the houses on the left were built by Mr Broadhurst of Burslem who named eight streets in his home town after his daughters. One of these houses, Laurance House, he named after one of his sons. The coach park is now on the right where Hollinedrakes Garage once stood. The boy pulling the handcart worked for the bootmakers, W. R. Hands of Wynnstay House, Conway Road.

42. (facing bottom) J. Bryn Jones & Kerman, Princes Drive, c.1925

This was a fruit and florist business located in the building which is now used as a Kentucky Fried Chicken franchise at 2 and 4 Princes Drive. A little further down the road, in Seaview Road, Mr J. H. Clegg was producing aerated water of all kinds in his patented 'Crown Cork Bottle' which he advertised as being a "boon to ladies' as there was no 'bursting of bottles' or 'escape of gas'.

41. Princess Cinema, c.1920

The Princess Cinema was built in 1914 and still stands, much changed with a totally new frontage, on Princes Drive. The little shop on the right is now a gentlemen's hairdressers (The Lox Box) and that on the left has now been incorporated into the cinema, which is now a bingo hall. The film showing at the time of the photograph was *The Face of the World* starring Bernard Bedford. The right hand end of this building can just be seen in picture No 38 in Volume 2.

43. Colwyn Bay Urban District Council Councillors and Staff, 1931-2

Photographed outside the old Council Offices on Conway Road (the building was demolished in the 1960s, see photograph No 51, Vol 2).

Front row (L-R): Dr W. McKendrick (Medical Officer of Health); Mr Adamson (chemist, Station Road); Miss Ethel M. Hovey, JP, CC; George Bevan; John Holman (Regent Shop, Conway Road); T. R. Davies (butcher); unknown; Mr Swindlehurst; Mr John Roberts (Dolwendy Stores, Llysfaen); A. Henry Salt (Mayor for two years); G. Pickstone.

Middle row (L-R): Unknown; Davy Edwards (Old Colwyn); J. Bewley; W. Meiwyn Jones; Oswald Jones, JP, CC; T. Arthur Hughes (solicitor & Mayor); Mr Jones Roberts (Free Library); unknown; Henry Parry, JP.

Back row (L-R): F. H. Porter (decorator, father of Charley Porter of the Metropole); Harry Blythe (gas engineer); Johnny Thomas (butcher); S. Colwyn Foulkes (see Vol 1 No 59); R. Bennett (Chief Financial officer); Walter Howarth (Mount Stewart Hotel); E. E. King (Charter Town Clerk 1934); Tommy Byron (estate agent); W. J. Dunning (Town Engineer & Surveyor); Mr Gregory (Pier Pavillion Manager); J. Glass (Parisian Café, Abergele Road); J. Lewis Jones (Chief Collector & Valuation Officer).

44. Colwyn Bay, 1960

The original Colwyn Bay Hotel can be seen at the bottom centre of this picture; it has since been demolished and the site is now occupied by the Princes Court flats. On the far side of the railway are, from L-R, Chester Engineering Garage, the allotments and Hollinedrake's Garage – all demolished to make way for the A55. In the centre right of the photograph is the Odeon Cinema which was demolished to make way for the Swn-y-Mor Retirement Apartments. The road running up from the junction, to the left of the Odeon, is Pwllycrochan Avenue which was once the driveway leading to Erskine House (now Rydal Junior School). At the top left can be seen Rydal Senior School and St John's Methodist Church, happily both still with us.

45. Rhiw Road, c.1910

There are four churches on Rhiw Road, three of which can be seen in this photograph – from L-R they are, Horeb Welsh methodist Chapel, St David's and St Paul's. The Union Church on Abergele Road can also be seen on the extreme right. The foundation stone of Horeb Chapel was laid in 1899 by Mrs Ellen Owen, the wife of William Owen who appears in Vol 2, picture No 66. In September 1950, the Chaired Bard, the Rev. Gwilym Tilsley, MA, took charge of the chapel.

46. Lancaster House, 1901

This building, now demolished, stood on Conway Road opposite the Midland Bank. To the right was The Mews from where J. Fred Francis ran his coach business. Mr T. Homan, the fancy goods dealer and Mr J. R. Jones were partners in Lancaster House. The local Post office was situated here for a while.

47. Abergele Road, 1907

The coach is stopped outside Buckley's Tea Rooms, the site now occupied by the National Westminster Bank

48. Colwyn Bay County School, Hockey 1st XI, 1935

Back row (L-R): Miss Lloyd; E. Evans; unknown; J. Munford; B. Evans; I. Howes.

Second row (L-R): B. Jones, unknown; A. Jones; Olive Gatley; J. Valentine.

Front: M. Hughes.

49. Roumania House, Station Road, c.1950

This building (now used by Lloyds Drugstore) stiil survives albeit minus the ornate verandah. It was the premises of A.S. Nevatt, gentlemen's outfitters. In 1899 it was the premises of Lewis & Thompson, drapers. The premises on the right are J. Wallis, boot and shoe dealer, another business which has disappeared.

50. Old Municipal Buildings, Station Road, c.1950

When erected in 1882, the door on the left was the entrance to the Police Station (there is a replica of a pair of handcuffs worked into the stone above the arch) and the window on the right hand corner was a door which led into the National Provincial Bank. The four terracotta plaques on the base of the spire depict the Colwyn Bay & Pwllcrochan Estate Co Ltd, the Seal of the Denbighshire County Constabulary, the National Provincial Bank of England Ltd and the Colwyn bay & Colwyn Local Board 1887. The ground floor was also once the offices of Porter & Amphlett (solicitors) and Booth, Chadwick & Porter (architects).

51. Ivy Street, c.1920

The buildings on the left are still mostly intact. The railway station can be seen in the distance. The cottages on the right have been demolished to make way for a car park. At the foot of the street was Rose Cottage. The town mortuary was half way down on the right. Ivy Street is the only 'street' in Colwyn bay and, in 1875, along with Station Road and Conway/Abergele Roads, formed one of the main thoroughfares in the town. The men are (L-R): Unknown; Andrew Jones, Bob Hurlston, Ted Lawton (killed in action over Belgium serving with the RAF) and Bill Foulkes.

52. Uxbridge House, Station Road, c.1945

This building now houses the Borough of Colwyn Information and Craft centre and is on the corner of Seaview Road and Station Road. Gilbeys premises on the left are now occupied by R.K.M. Wools. Frank Little's business, run by Mr John Bowler, is fondly remembered because of the nostalgic smell of roasted coffee which permeated the shop and which now lingers only in the mind.

![Abergele Road photograph]

53. Abergele Road, c.1920
The old F. W. Woolworth building is sited behind the trees middle left. The open, single-decker tram was known as a 'toast-rack' because of its appearance. The *Royal Hotel* is on the right.

54. Parry & Jones, Woodland Road East, 1906
The plumbers, Parry & Jones' workshop and showroom was situated more or less between what is now Woolworths and the former premises of Osborns (solicitors). The back of the town library can be seen on the left and was built in 1905.

55. 'A' Coy, 2nd RWF Cadet Battalion, August 1949

L-R: E. Jones, D. Roberts, T. E. Owen, Cpl C. Jones, L Cpl L. Y. Head. These cadets have just passed their Part 1 Certificate A at Kinmel Camp and are photographed at the RWF Gun Park, Princes Drive. Two Nissen huts from the park survive opposite the Hopeside Hotel until June 1997. This is now the site of the King's Court development.

56. Marine Road, 22 June 1911

A procession celebrating the Coronation of King George V and Queen Mary, pass down Marine Road towards the junction with Princes Drive before moving on to the promenade.

57. May Day, 1920

On 5 May, 1920, the May Queen and members of her Court, pause for a photograph in front of the Town Hall, the buildings in the background being in Wynnstay Road, with the roof of the present day Royal Bank of Scotland being behind the tram line post. Following the parade, there was an evening show at the Pier Pavillion with seventeen separate items on the bill, the final one being the 'Exit of the May Queen and Court'.

The Drummer Boys are (L-R): Cyril Hunt, Ken Neil, B. Cheshire, Alan Neil, Christopher Newall Jones, unknown, Eric Holt, Joe Cheshire and Bobby Lamb. Seated in the car are (L-R): the May Queen, Miss Marjorie Eileen Chant Owen, Gwenny Pattison, Clifford Arundale, Albert Braid (driver), Charles Porter (Trumpeter Charley, later of the Metropole Hotel).

58. Brooklands, c.1890

A photograph showing the rural nature of Colwyn Bay during the early days of its development. The building on the right is now 34 Brackley Avenue (Brooklands); there are now two other large houses located behind this called Coed Helyg and Haddon Lodge. The photograph was taken from roughly where Oak Drive is today. With the exception of the area behind the trees on the right (where Rydal School has two rugger pitches), between Lansdowne Road and Conway Road, these fields are now filled with houses. Extreme left is the St Enoch's Hotel and, in the middle of the picture, are the backs of the houses on Penrhyn Road.

59. Visit of the Prince of Wales, 1923

A photograph taken on the Promenade on 2 November 1923. The figures are (L-R): Capt E. J. Meredith (Meredith & Kirkham Garage, Old Colwyn), the Prince of Wales (later the Duke of Windsor), Sir Henry Morris Jones (wearing a top hat), Lord Kenyon, unknown First World War veteran. Miss Louisa Greenfield, a teacher at Douglas Road School, recalls having to keep the children occupied as the Prince, having extended a lunch engagement in Llandudno, was late arriving.

60. Hydropathic Establishment, 1893

This building was used as a centre where guests could take a holiday and improve their health at the same time. In 1895 it became the home of Penrhos College when the Medicine Room corridor and the small rooms off it were transformed into classrooms for the lower forms and the Turkish bath section became a cloak room and piano practice room. Penrhos College was founded on 27 September 1880 under the auspices of the Wesleyan Methodist Church and was originally housed in Gilbertville on the Promenade. Miss Wenn was the first Principal and Miss Martin the first Matron, in charge of twelve girls and two pupil teachers. There was no school uniform and the girls were allowed to wear large silver lockets and chains. In 1896 the fees were 2 guineas per term.

61. Pier Pavillion, 1933

A photograph taken on 17 May 1933, the morning after the disastrous fire. The Bijou Pavillion at the pierhead was burnt down on 28 July of the same year. The official opening of the third and present pavillion took place on 8 May 1934 (see Vol 1 No. 44 and Vol 2, No. 23),

62. Henry William Pegler, c.1900

Henry Pegler was one of Colwyn Bay's early official postmen as evidence the number on his collar. A story still survives that, as the state of his teeth deteriorated in later life, he began to ask the residents of the mansions on Tan-y-Bryn Road (which was part of his round) for donations towards a set of false teeth! His son was the commis-sionaire of the Princes Cinema in Princes Drive.

63. Alfred Langdon Coburn, 1882-1966

Alfred Coburn was one of the foremost and most accomplished photographers of this century. Sir Tom Hopkinson, Editor of *Picture Post* called him "a giant amongst giants", while George Bernard Shaw referred to him as one of "the most sensitive artist-photographers now living". Born in Boston, USA, he came to live at Awen, 17 Ebberston Road East, Rhos-on-Sea in 1945. He and his wife are buried in Llandrillo-yn-Rhos churchyard. This photograph is a self portrait, entitled 'The Copper Plate Process' and published in 1908.

64. Conway Road Board School, 1888

Front row: 4th from left, Will Greenfield, 5th from left, David Greenwood, 6th from left Lillie Greenfield. A fourth member of this family, Louisa (not in the photograph) is still living in Colwyn Bay aged 106. She can remember walking along a narrow lane from her home in Colwyn Bay to the school at the West End. The lane is now the main Conway Road.

65. Llanrwst Road, c.1920

The houses on the left are now Nos 147 and 149 Farmside and the building on the right has become the Hindhead Country Hotel. This was one of the ancient roads leading out of Colwyn Bay, in this case to Bryn-y-Maen and the Holland Arms (see No. 66). Both sides of the road are now lined with dwellings.

66. Holland Arms, c.1910

This is the 17th century coaching house located on crossroads of the Llangernyw, Llanrwst, Eglwysbach and Colwyn Bay roads. On the sign of *The White Lion* public house at Llanelian can still be seen the rampant lion of the Holland family of Teyrdan. Water for this establishment was drawn from local wells and pack animals were the commonplace style of transport for goods along this road; a string of donkeys might have been seen bearing panniers filled with merchandise, or kegs containing drinking water. Although stage-coaches had been replaced by the railways as modes of passenger transport in the mid-19th century, they were still in regular use during the early years of the 20th century, particularly for special excursions such as those operated by Fred Francis of Colwyn Bay.

67. Francis Garage, New Branch Mews, 1900

This is the rear of what was, until recently, the local Ford Garage at West End which opens on to Carlton Road. It was built by Fred Francis (see Vol. 2 No. 19). Fred's son, Jim, who is on the left of the photograph, started and ran a riding school at the top of Rhos Road. The buildings seen here still survive but the courtyard has been covered and was used as a car paint spray shop.

68. J. Fred Francis & Sons, Garage, 1922

This was the 'new mews' garage in the countryside built to compliment the establishments in Penrhyn Road and Conway Road. The garage is now empty and the photograph was taken before the shops and flats were built opposite the forecourt. In the background can be seen Brickfield Terrace which was demolished to make way for the A55.

69. Nant Smithy, c.1895

The view looking down Llanrwst Road to Conway Road which runs left to right. The old Tan–Bryn bridge in the background was roughly where the present footbridge spans the A55 and railway. The smithy building was demolished when the railway track was doubled.

70. Mochdre Post Office, c.1920

A view of Conway Road leading towards Colwyn Bay with Bryn Euryn in the background. The Post office was the house on the right, behind the tree, now called Duffryn. The present wrought-iron gate of Duffryn is all that remains of the Eagle Farm. The fields on the left are now the site of Mochdre Garage, Bryn Marl Road and the Council housing estate.

71. The Bay of Colwyn, c.1906

To the right is the growing community of Colwyn Bay while on the left can be seen the first houses to be built on Whitehall Road. The copse of trees in the centre is roughly where the 'five ways' roundabout is today. The tents house army Volunteer units on manouvres.

72. Mochdre Mayday, 1946

The ceremony held in fields now covered by Ffordd Gobaith, Eryr, Euryn, Cwstenin etc. The buildings just visible middle left are on Singleton Crescent.

73. Dinerth Road and Bryn Euryn, c.1925

This photograph was taken from roughly the present site of the Colwyn Bay Rugby Club ground. The fields are now covered by the houses on Crafnant Road, Bodnant Road, Cambrian Drive, Brookfield Drive and Craig View. A German aeroplane dropped three bombs on this field on 7 April 1941, causing damage to a small footbridge.

74. Penrhyn View, Rhos-on-Sea, c.1910

Now known as Dinerth Road, this street was originally called Penrhyn View because the houses looked across the fields towards Penrhynside. The houses on the left are now Nos 163–73 and look up Princess Avenue. Those on the right are (R-L) Nos 162–80.

75. Rhos-on-Sea, 1911

This photograph was taken soon after the pier had been erected and shows Bryn Euryn on the left. The conical building at the end of the pier is now part of Rhos Point Café.

76. Comberemere Lodge, Rhos Promenade, c.1890

Comberemere Lodge (behind the steam roller) was demolished about 1900 and was sited where the information kiosk now stands opposite the Cayley Arms (which can be seen on the right –then known as The Blue Bell Inn).

77. Allanson Road Bowling Club Outing, 1935

The club members are photographed at Betws-y-coed. The lady on the right is Mrs Beardsall and the lady seated on the left is Mrs Polly Roberts whose husband Percy is standing in the centre looking straight at the camera (they are the parents of the Captain of the Rhos College Cricket Team shown in Vol 1, No 65).

78. Llys Euryn, 1906

The cast of the Llandrillo Church production of Ednyfed Fychan, written by the vicar, Rev E James Evans. The cast members are (L-R): Gladys Tozer, Doris Roberts, Mr Bostock (of Bod Euryn), unknown, unknown, the Darlington sisters (from the *Cayley Arms*), Rev Evans, unknown, unknown, Hughie Gale (butcher), unknown, unknown, Johnny Walker (cowman at Bryn Euryn Farm). Front: Arthur Owen Roberts, Effie Tozer.

79. Penrhyn Avenue, 1935

Eddie Beardsall (standing) and Stanley Hoskins changing a tyre on an Austin 12. In the background is the Rhos-on-Sea Playhouse which is now the Co-op shop. Penrhyn Avenue was originally called Tramway Avenue because it took the line laid out for the trams.

82. Swimming Pool, Rhos-on-Sea, c.1956

The Swimming Pool, open only in the summer months, was situated behind the Rhos Abbey Hotel and the Creggin-y-Mynach public house, on the site now developed as gardens. The entrance was in Abbey Road. Mr Breeze was the manager and he would pay John Taylor, John Williams and Master Timewell (known as 'Timebomb') 2/6d each to twice weekly black up their faces, hang a board on their backs and cycle along the Promenade, through Eirias Park and back to Rhos to advertise the twice weekly Crazy Nights; they also had to perform (for no extra money) in the evening shows. Mr Breeze used to put the water temperatures on a board each day, all the locals being quite convinced that several degrees were added to entice the faint-hearted into the water. On one occasion, Mrs Nock, a lady who ran one of the shops in the pool precinct, noticed a local swimmer, Emlyn Pierce, shivering in the water. She asked him if he was cold and, on being assured that he thought the water colder than advertised, she went into her shop and boiled a kettle of water which she then poured into the pool, explaining to Emlyn that he should now feel a lot warmer.